THE BRONZE SERPENT

*Tethering Your Life to the Cross
with Scripture-Based Prayer*

. . . .

Dr. McKay Caston

For my Savior, Jesus

"to the praise of your glorious grace"

May you live
all of life in view
of the cross!

Melby Caster

"And as Moses lifted up the serpent in the wilderness, so must the Son of Man be lifted up, that whoever believes in him may have eternal life."

John 3:14-15

Table of Contents

Preface

There are many books on prayer and many books centering on Bible study. My desire in this effort was to join the two: the Bible *and* prayer. Therefore, you will notice that each prayer is also a theological and practical reflection on a particular passage of Scripture. My goal was to let the Bible inform my conversations with God, turning prayer into a dialogue that centers on my need to live completely in dependence upon the grace of God—in view of the cross.

As I walked through this project, the image that continued to stand out in my mind was the bronze serpent of Numbers 21. The Israelites grumbled against the Lord and his representative, Moses, and as an act of judgment, the Lord sent poisonous snakes to invade the camp. Many people were bitten and died. As an act of mercy upon his people, he instructed Moses to construct a pole, and to put a bronze serpent upon it. The serpents remained a threat, but now, when someone was bitten, he or she could look upon the raised serpent upon the pole and be healed.

In John 3:14-15, Jesus applies that image to himself, saying that he is the One to whom sin-bit sinners should look for their healing—for their forgiveness and reconciliation with God. That is why he was raised up on a cross, *to be a substitute*. He took the venom and died so that we, through gazing upon the cross in faith, might be forgiven of sin and imputed with the antidote of his righteousness.

My motive in these prayers is to know God through his word and through spiritual conversation so that I might more deeply and fully experience his grace. I trust that these prayers, by the power of the Holy Spirit, will enable you to share in that experience.

My suggestion is that, as you read, you use these prayers as kindling for your own conversations with our Abba, Father. My prayer for you is that weaving Scripture and prayer will provide you with a style of prayer that is Biblical, theological, relational, practical and most importantly, tied and tethered to the message of grace in the gospel of Jesus.

McKay Caston
Dahlonega, Georgia

The Presence and Power of God

"Have I not commanded you? Be strong and courageous.
Do not be terrified; do not be discouraged, for the LORD
your God will be with you wherever you go."
Joshua 1:9

. . . . ●●●●●●● . . . .

My Father and my God, when you instructed Joshua to
be strong and courageous as he led your people into the
land of promise, you assured him that you would be with
him. He would not be alone and would not do battle in his
own power. His strength and courage were to grow in his
heart not because of *his* greatness, but because of *yours*.

Only a river separated him from a nation that, on
paper, he had no chance of defeating. Surely, he would
question his call to such a seemingly impossible task. Even
as Peter looked at the waves and found himself sinking, so
Joshua would be tempted to look at the enemy and lose

heart. But you told him that you would be with him. Your presence and power would sustain him. So, he was commanded to be strong and courageous—a strength and courage that would have to flow from faith.

Father, as I consider your call on my life, I know that your Spirit is instructing me with the same command: *be strong and courageous.* I do not face Canaanites, but I do face other enemies and other challenges that feel just as overwhelming. Each one requires no less faith in your presence and power than it took Joshua to lead Israel over the river to fight. You were with him and have promised to be with me...even *in* me.

Yet the most significant aspect of Joshua's command does not apply to me, but to you, Jesus. You are the ultimate Joshua. As Moses was used to deliver the Israelites from the enemy in Egypt and as Joshua was to lead the people against another enemy in Canaan, you have faced sin and death and proved faithful in victory. Jesus, it is your strength and courage in the cross that has saved me. Apart from your Spirit within me, I am all weakness and fear.

How desperately I need your presence and power, and how I thank you that it is available in the gospel. Yes, having such a strong and courageous Savior gives me the faith from which my own weakness is turned into strength and in which my fear gives way to courage.

Father, this day I will face people who will intimidate and circumstances that will overwhelm. May I know your presence and power. Your presence to fill me with a sense of your love and acceptance, and your power to give me the ability to believe, to repent, to encourage, to listen, to confront, to love, to forgive, to persevere, to hope and to pray.

Yes, I am utterly dependent upon your grace. Your grace that saves and your grace that enables me now to follow where you lead. Because Jesus was forsaken in my place, I will never be forsaken. You will always be with me wherever I go. Help me to be so mindful of that wonderful promise. Let me never feel alone, but always, and especially today, know your presence and your power.

The Love of God

"You see, at just the right time, when we were still powerless, Christ died for the ungodly... God demonstrates his love for us in this: while we were still sinners, Christ died for us."

Romans 5:6, 8

· · · · · · · · · ● ● ● ● ● ● ● · · · · · · · · ·

Father in heaven, you love me. Yes, *you* love *me*. Though I confess that saying those words does not come easily for me, for I know how unlovely and unlovable I really am. As your word says, I am ungodly. In my flesh, I am utterly unable, powerless to do anything that would cause a holy God to love me. It is so hard to believe that your love for me could possibly be unwavering. Yet this perspective comes from a heart that misunderstands love, and thus, has misunderstood you.

When I love, it is often in response to good behavior, beauty or some form of success or accomplishment. I lavish affection on those who are lovely and lovable. The result is that my love is not love at all; it is reward. I assume that you love in the same way.

How I thank you that you are teaching me that your love is *not* reward. It is *grace*. Your word tells me that you have loved me from before the foundation of the world. You knew that I would be an ungodly sinner, and yet you set your affection on me. I was not lovely, but you loved me. You have demonstrated your love for me in this: that while I was unlovable, you gave Jesus to die for me. Peter says that Christ died for my sins once and for all, the righteous dying for the unrighteous, to bring me to God.

You did not wait for me to become beautiful in your sight before you loved me. In fact, it is your love for me that now has *made* me beautiful. In the cross, Jesus has taken away my ugliness and has made me perfectly righteous in your sight. I am no longer defined by my sin, but rather, I am defined by your love. How I worship you for such a transforming grace!

Father, it was Augustine who said that the cross of Christ did not secure the love of God, but that it was your love for sinners like me that secured the cross. You were not talked into loving me or obligated because of the cross. The cross is that which tells me what lengths you went to reconcile a wayward son and to bring him home so that I can know your love and be convinced of it.

My prayer today is that, with the apostle Paul, I would know the height, depth, width and breadth of your love for me in Jesus. Yet, as the heavens surpass my ability to understand them, so does the cross. And yet, Paul's prayer is that I would have the supernatural ability to grasp it—at least in part. So by the grace of your indwelling Spirit, flood my heart with an palpable sense of your kindness, your mercy, and yes, your love for me, so that I will be able to love others, not as a reward, but as a gift of grace.

In View of God's Mercy

"Therefore, I urge you, brothers, in view of God's mercy,
to offer your bodies as living sacrifices, holy and
pleasing to God— this is your
spiritual act of worship."

Romans 12:1

· · · · · • • • • • ● ● ● • • • • • • · · ·

Abba, Father, why should I need to be urged to offer myself to you as a living sacrifice? In view of your mercy, why should I not be compelled to worship you with the totality of my being, in every moment and circumstance? As Jeremiah says, your mercies are new every morning— even in the face of the most terrible suffering and brokenness. Maybe even *especially* in the face of suffering and brokenness.

Someone has said that the problem with a living sacrifice is that it is always trying to get off the altar. I suppose that is true. It is so hard to follow your ways. Humility. Repentance. Faith. Suffering. Trials. Ridicule. Peer pressure. It wasn't even easy for you, Jesus. When faced with the physical, emotional and spiritual pain required by the cross, you asked if there was another way. But in the face of the calling to sacrifice yourself, you delighted in the will of the Father and gave yourself without regret to the hardest of all obediences.

It is there that I discover your mercy. Whatever trial I am called to face, it will never have to be the ultimate trial. Even as I share in your sufferings, I am not contributing to your sufferings. Every tear and wave of grief reminds me of the tribulation you endured on my behalf, reconciling an unloving sinner to a loving God.

In view of that mercy, and the multifaceted mercies that surround my life every day, I do want to offer myself to you. Asking that you would fill me with your presence and power so that a weak and broken vessel like me might be a living testimony to your greatness and grace. I want to give you my eyes, that what I view will please you. I long for a will that desires to be in accord with your will, and your heart. How I want the eyes of Jesus! To see even as you see.

I want to possess the gift of listening to others in a way that I enter their story and am able to lead them to their heart's true desire, which is to know and experience you. But not only the eyes and ears, I long for the mouth of Jesus so that I would speak words of life, compassion, truth and grace. Speaking not in a way that boasts in myself, but one that leads people to the same cross where I have found my life.

I also want the hands of Jesus. Hands that fulfill my vocation in a way that is done unto the Lord, and not merely unto man. Whether people see it or not, whether they praise it or not, may I give my work to you, since as an act of grace, you have given it to me.

Yet I confess that offering my life to you in these ways does not come naturally. This will require the supernatural work of your Spirit, to keep me on the altar when my flesh so desperately wants to escape. Let me find joy in submission and obedience, knowing that it is not only good for me, but pleases you.

Let me then experience a life of worship. A life of honoring the God who gave life to the dead and hope to the hopeless. This is the life of grace I crave, living in view of your mercy.

Not Ashamed

"I am not ashamed of the gospel, for it is the power of God for the salvation to everyone who believes."

Romans 1:16a

. . . .

Abba, Father, and God of my salvation, Paul was not ashamed of the gospel. He knew it was powerful, and when ignited by your Spirit, it would bring total, transforming change to those who received it. He knew that the gospel is the message that brings people out of the kingdom of darkness and into the kingdom of light, delivers people from death to life, and transforms them from condemned enemies to beloved sons and daughters.

Your gospel is the message of your grace to sinners, telling people like me that, in the life, death and resurrection of Jesus, you have done for me what I could not do for myself. Jesus has fulfilled the law in my place.

He has endured the judgement that I deserved. He has given me life that I did not earn. He came to serve me and to save me, opening the door for me to enjoy you as you intended from the beginning. All to magnify your glory as a God of grace.

What a glorious gospel!

On one hand I am sure that Paul shared the gospel because he had been commissioned. You called him to be an apostle—one who is sent with a message. And yet a motive deeper than mere obligation compelled him to share the gospel so freely, and often, under very difficult circumstances, having been persecuted severely, and ultimately losing his physical life for not being ashamed of the gospel.

In one of his letters, Paul says that it was the love of Jesus that compelled him. Even though knew he possessed a message of spiritual dynamite that needed to be released, I think it was the powerful effect that the gospel had had on him that drove him to testify, even as a martyr, to your glory in the gospel. He had been saved by the same Jesus whom he proclaimed. As some have said, there is a propulsion to grace—those whom receive grace begin to extend it to others.

If that is true, and if I claim to have experienced the saving power of the gospel in my own life, then why do I appear to be ashamed of it? Why am I so slow to speak of the gospel? And when I do, why am I sharing from the intellectual surface of my heart instead of the emotional depths? Why am I more impassioned to speak about my favorite sports team, a current event or even my computer's new operating system than I am to speak about the grace of Jesus?

Father, I confess that I have felt ashamed, and I am so sorry. I don't want to be ashamed. Rather, I want to have the passion of the apostle, who knew himself to be the worst of sinners and an example to others concerning what it meant for God to justify the ungodly, people like him and me who turn to anything and everything apart from Jesus to save us.

What I need is not more commitment. In order not to be ashamed of the gospel and to share it freely and with passion, I need to personally re-experience your grace at a deep level—at a level that will ignite my soul with a desire for others to experience your grace, so that you will become the object of their joy.

Gracious Father, will you enable me this day to be so filled with your love that I overflow with a desire to share it? Then you will be glorified by one who is compelled by your love to extend your love.

Godly Sorrow

*"Godly sorrow brings repentance that leads to salvation
and leaves no regret, but worldly sorrow leads to death."*

2 Corinthians 7:10

· · · · · · · · ● ● ● ● ● ● ● · · · · · · · ·

Father of grace, I pray that the sadness in my heart
would be godly rather than worldly sorrow. That I would
be broken over seeking my joy and life in other things
beside yourself. As you challenged the people of Israel
through Jeremiah so long ago, you also challenge me, that
I have dug cisterns that can hold no water. I have sought to
find my joy in reputation, success, physical comfort, and so
many other shallow resources.

Jesus, you tell me that you are the river of living water.
It is deep and wide, and thoroughly satisfying. Yet I dig
wells in the desert, hoping, even straining, to discover a
taste of satisfaction and joy in other, lesser pursuits.

Sometimes it appears as if I have found it, but it is always a temporary pleasure, unlike the eternal joy that is found simply in knowing you and experiencing your presence.

By your grace, you rescue me from myself as your Holy Spirit brings godly sorrow into my heart. A sorrow from God and unto God. A sorrow that you create in my heart that longs to be reconciled to you, Father, to follow you and to glorify you.

I come to repent, to be honest about the reality of my sin nature and my propensity to follow it away from you, the source of life, to dig wells. I confess my cold-heartedness. How I want to be on fire and experience a passion for your presence!

That is where repentance leads, isn't it? Repentance takes me to the cross, where my Savior bears the burden of justice for my well-digging, cold-heartedness, and every other conceivable deviation that my life has taken from your will and your ways. He says, "It is finished," and you call me your beloved son. Forgiven. Accepted. Treasured. Never to be forsaken.

My heart is beginning to understand that the gospel is not religion. It is not about what I can do for you, but what you have done for me. It is about the Gift. The undeserved, unearned gift of knowing you and experiencing your presence as my Father.

As your word says, *perfect love casts out fear*. And so,

when I can fully embrace, and be embraced by the truth of your gospel for me, I can begin to grow with a passion for your presence. To know you. To love you. To glorify you. That is the goal of my salvation, and why the grace of godly sorrow leads to it. And that is why, Father, there is no regret in the pain of repentance. Because I learn that through Jesus' pain, I am redeemed and adopted, forgiven and loved. Treasured, not merely tolerated.

Father, I pray that I would experience this godly sorrow, and be wise not to mistake it for worldly sorrow. Worldly sorrow is the sorrow of Judas, whose sin nature cast him into despair, condemning him and convincing him that there was no hope.

When I see my sin, enable me not to fix my eyes on it, but rather on the blood of Jesus. Deliver me from despair and fill me with the hope of the gospel so that I may experience a new desire to love, follow and glorify you, Father, Son and Spirit. To that end, my repentance will never have any regret.

Adopted by God

"For he chose us in him before the creation of the world to be holy and blameless in his sight. In love he predestined us to be adopted as his sons through Jesus Christ, in accordance with his pleasure and will—to the praise of his glorious grace, which he has freely given us in the One he loves."

Ephesians 1:3-6

. . . . ●●●● ●●● ● ● ● . . . . .

Abba Father, why is it that you adopted me? I know it was not my goodness or moral purity. It was not my intellect or ability to serve in some great capacity in your kingdom. When I reflect upon who I am in relation to your majesty, I am overwhelmed with how utterly unworthy I am to be associated with Jesus.

Yet he is pleased to call me his brother, and you, Father, are delighted to call me your son. This is because you chose to adopt me as a son as an act of mercy, "to the praise of your glorious grace!" Yes, I am unworthy. Your kindness to me is undeserved. But you have set your love upon me before the creation of the world and proven it by sending Jesus to pay the adoption price on the cross.

I have been rescued from the kingdom of darkness and delivered unto the kingdom of light. I am now a citizen of heaven with the full rights of a son of God. Full rights! Amazing! As a child of a king has access to the epicenter of power and rule over a nation, so I have access to the King of all creation.

Why then do I live on so many days as if I were a spiritual orphan with no Abba? Why am I so insecure? Why do I crave approval and praise and need affirmation from peers and those of significance so badly? Me, a son of the King, concerned about what others think of me. How can this be?

How can I worry like I do? How can a son of the King live in fear of the future or with regret over the past, knowing that his Father-King oversees the lives of his sons and daughters, guiding them and working in and through them for their good? Not so much so that they get what they want, but that they get what they need, which is more of the grace that comes through Jesus.

When I am unaware that being near to you in your presence, Jesus, is my great need, I forget the gospel, and begin seeking a name for myself rather than magnifying your name as my Savior, Friend, and Brother. Forgive me of such self-oriented sin that causes that orphan spirit to grow within my heart.

To this end you have given me your Spirit, so that I may cry out, "Abba, Father." He is the Spirit of adoption who enables me to remember *who* I am, and *whose* I am. I have been declared by the King to be his holy, blameless, and dearly loved, child—from before the creation of the world. No, it was not for my goodness that I was adopted. It was an expression of your grace and love. Help me cry out even today for more of your Spirit to indwell me and to show me Jesus—*to the praise of your glory!*

The Ways of the Lord

"For my thoughts are not your thoughts, neither are your ways my ways, declares the Lord. For as the heavens are higher than the earth, so are my ways higher than your ways and my thoughts than your thoughts."
Isaiah 55:8-9

· · · · · · · · · · ●●●●●●● · · · · · · · · · ·

Abba, Father, the Spirit within me rejoices in your sovereign rule over all people, places, and events. The wisdom with which you execute your providence is perfect. The knowledge that you are not only in control but are also actively are guiding the flow of history with knowledge and purpose is a resource that you intend to provide peace and hope in my life.

However, I confess that I struggle to embrace your ways. In my foolish finiteness, I believe that I have a better plan for my life and your world. Yet even you, Jesus, understand. Not the foolishness or finiteness, but the struggle. In the garden of Gethsemane, you knew the pathway of pain that lay before you in the cross, and asked the Father is there was another way. You knew the answer, but in your humanity, you manifested that you can empathize with having to willingly submit to the ways of the Father.

Willingly submit. That is a lesson that I need to learn. I need to believe that your ways are wise, full of eternal knowledge, and are perfect. Even if they involve the sins of others, pain, and suffering. Even if I do not understand. Even if I think my ways would reflect a greater wisdom. Forgive me for such arrogance and shortsightedness. I simply cannot fathom the contingencies surrounding every event, wind, tide and circumstance. It is a burden too great for me to bear and is likely the cause of much of my stress and anxiety. I am trying to be my own lord and to wear a crown that only you can wear rightly and effectively.

You tell me that your thoughts and ways are far beyond my understanding. In fact, Paul asks the rhetorical question, "For who has known the mind of the Lord, or who has been his counselor?" I confess that I have wanted to provide my counsel. I have a plan for my life in my mind. A plan that is free of suffering and challenge. A life that is comfortable. A life that is free of having to believe, follow and rest in the ways of another.

Father, I thank you that "another" is not a distant, capricious God of fate, but rather is my Abba, the God of grace. Yes, you are my Sovereign Father. My prayer today is that you would enable me to know you so deeply that I can trust you more fully. Empower me to rest in you as my Savior God to such a degree that I will be able to rest in you as my sovereign God as well.

Allow me to experience the gift of humility and submission. Help me confess the ignorance of my ways and embrace the wisdom of yours. Give me eyes to see you as the King, ruling and working all things for your glory and for my good, and ultimate joy. Let all things be means of grace in my life. All things. So that you might be glorified through all seasons of my life, whether that of singing and dancing or sadness and pain.

The Blessed Life

"Blessed is the one whose transgression is forgiven,
whose sin is covered."

Psalm 32:1

. . . . ● ● ● ● ● ● ● ● . . . .

My God and refuge, who has paid the debt of my sin. You tell me that the *blessed* life is the *forgiven* life. It is the blessing of having a God express his grace by sending his own son to remove the sins of his people. Father, how I thank you for being that God, and Jesus, for being such a Savior who has made atonement for my willful and wicked transgression.

Lord Jesus, the Scriptures describe what you did on the cross as the bearing of a curse. You received my justice. You served my sentence. You paid my debt. And you have blessed me with an eternal grace that flows from your eternal love. Let me never take such a blessing for granted or consider it in any way secondary to what my flesh considers a blessing.

For my flesh sees the blessed life as the wealthy life. The successful life. The life filled with many possessions. And when others appear to have more, my heart grows jealous and filled with discontent. I covet and become cold to the spiritual blessings of the gospel. Why do I so often translate blessing in material and financial terms, when your Word warns against the love of possessions. As your word says, "It is through this craving that some have wandered away from the faith and pierced themselves with many pangs."

May I remember that you were pierced for me! May I prize as priceless your precious, efficacious blood. You are the pearl of great price, and the gospel is my great possession. Promises for now and eternity. An inheritance kept in heaven that can never spoil or fade. Riches of grace to be bestowed forever. I am wealthy beyond the wildest imagination! Thank you, Jesus! Give me eyes to see the practical significance of the blessed life that is covered by your atoning sacrifice, that has reconciled me to God and guaranteed blessing upon blessing, now and forever.

Father, as one who has been forgiven, enable me, as one of the blessed, to be a blessing to others. I want to be one who forgives—one who pays down the debts of others against me. How I desire the ability to set others free, living as a conduit of grace for the praise of your glory. But this can only come from your indwelling Spirit. My flesh is still so strong in my heart. I find myself harboring grudges and growing in bitterness toward those who are my debtors. Yet Jesus, the prayer you taught me assumes that I, having been blessed with forgiveness, will be one who blesses others with forgiveness.

How I need more grace. I thank you that your blood has covered every single sin, especially the hardened places in my heart that are still slow to forgive. As you demonstrated on the cross, Jesus, forgiveness involves pain. It is not easy to forgive, for the price is high. It may be free for the recipient, but the cost is steep for the one who pays down the debt. That is why it is so hard, and why I think it is a supernaturally empowered gift that you give in order to let your grace flow *from* the cross, *to* me, and *through* me. But when the grace flows, there is joy in the blessing, as there was Jesus when you, for the joy set before you, endured the cross.

Father, my prayer today is that, in being so richly, overwhelmingly blessed, I would be supernaturally empowered by your Holy Spirit to be a blessing by re-gifting forgiveness and passing on the blessed life.

A New Creation

"If anyone is in Christ, he is a new creation. The old has passed away; behold, the new has come."

2 Corinthians 5:17 (ESV)

· · · · · · · ● ● ● ● ● ● ● · · · · · · · · ·

Abba, can it really be true that I am a new creation? Is the significance of your Spirit in me that profound—that I'm a new person? Totally new? When I reflect upon the years, I realize that I once was blind to my need of a Savior, but now I see. I once was deaf to the voice of my shepherd, but now I hear. I once was dead to a love for God, but now I have new affections. I once was condemned in my sin, but now I have been set free through the cross. I once lived without hope, but now I have an eternal inheritance of glory to experience and enjoy. Yes, new! New eyes. New ears. New affections. New peace. New hope. All is *new*! Oh, how I praise and worship you for the gift of the new creation! "The old has passed away; behold, the new has come."

Yet, as I reflect upon this verse, I have a question. Could it be that Paul is weaving together several aspects of the new creation? Or might there be various strands to unweave in order to understand why the old has passed but still wreaks havoc in my life? Is it possible that Paul is speaking of regeneration, justification, *and* sanctification in one bundle?

By virtue of the Spirit's regenerating grace, I am a new creation who has been given new eyes and ears—eyes and ears that lead me to repentance and faith. Then, having confessed my sins and received your forgiveness, I am justified. Legally, the old man has been crucified and condemned at the cross, and by virtue of your gospel declaration, I am now counted as righteous in your sight because of the merits of Jesus credited to me.

Father, this is where I think that the sanctification part comes in. You have definitively pronounced me holy. Justified. However, you have told me through the same apostle that I am to *continually* put off the old self and put on the new. On one hand it is a declaration (my justification) and on the other it is a process (my sanctification). That explains why the old self sometimes seems to be so alive and destructive in my life. It blinds my eyes to the truth and deafens my ears to your voice.

It deceives me with alternate affections, and when I fall, it condemns, seeking to convince me that I could never be a beloved son of the Father.

That is why I pray for ears that will be able to listen to your word, which tells me that the old self was crucified with Jesus in order that my sinful nature might be brought to nothing, so that I will not be enslaved to sin. So that is what I need. Ears to hear the gospel. Eyes to see the cross— the bronze serpent who has healed my wounds and forgiven my sin. *There is no more condemnation!* Then, in believing my justification I will be free to pursue sanctification by abiding in the righteousness of Jesus and, by the grace and power of the Holy Spirit, manifesting his fruit.

Father, as your new creation, let my eyes see, my ears hear, my heartbeat and my feet walk in response to the wonder of your glorious grace.

Born of God

"But to all who did receive him, who believed in his name, he gave the right to become children of God, who were born, not of blood nor of the will of the flesh nor of the will of man, but of God."

John 1:12-13

· · · · · · · · · · ● ● ● ● ● ● ● · · · · · · · · · ·

My God and giver of life, that is what I must do in order to be your child. I must *receive*. I cannot work, earn or merit my adoption. It is a gift that must be received through faith alone. What priceless grace it is to know that I am one of those who have received Jesus. I have received the forgiveness of sins and the righteousness of the Savior!

Father, I delight that this is all of grace. As your word says so clearly: I was dead in my sins and an object of wrath. But because of the greatness of your love, you, who are full of mercy, made me alive. Sovereignly, not as a duty or obligation to any merit in me, but out of sheer grace, you gave me new life. Regeneration. Spiritual resurrection.

That resurrection of spiritual life has enabled me to have new eyes and ears. Now, I can hear your Spirit call. I hear him convict, and I hear him convince me that the gospel is true. Father, I am learning that regeneration is the source of my repentance and faith. For how would I have seen myself to be a wretched sinner in need of mercy without the new eyes that your Spirit has given?

Yes, my being a child of God is all of grace. So why do I grow proud? Why do I live so often as if I have been born into the kingdom as the result of my own spiritual, intellectual, or moral merits? Why do I act as if there were something commendable in me that caused you to choose me? Why do I look down upon those who are blind and deaf to spiritual things? I confess the arrogance of my flesh. I confess that in my sinful nature, I am blind to your grace and deaf to your kindness.

I pray that you would convict me afresh of the indwelling sin that refuses to live in the humble place—the sin that wants to be king of the hill. Remind me that the ground is level at the foot of the cross, where all kinds of sinners gather, as if in the same sinking boat, to receive the gift of rescue and salvation in the person of Jesus.

Your word says that all fall short of your glory, and that all are saved in the same way, with the same need for the propitiation of Jesus' blood. Jesus, forgive me for being the Pharisee in Luke 18. Rather, may I be the man who went away from the temple justified, not because his prayer was so good or life so exemplary, but because he knew himself to be *the* sinner, not just *a* sinner. He knew that he needed the gospel *personally*, not just *theoretically*.

Today, I want to experience the gospel personally. I want to remember that I have been born again as a result of your will and not my own. I am a son by sheer grace. My rights as a son have been granted as a gift. But they are rights, nonetheless. Rights to rest in the work of Jesus. Rights to come before you as my Abba. Rights to trust you as my King. Rights to share the good news to other sinners, who by grace, will come into the family because you have set your eternal, fatherly love upon them, too. Thank you, Abba, Father, for being such a saving, rescuing, adopting, and loving God.

Rest for the Weary

"Come unto me, all you who are weary and burdened,
and I will give you rest."
Matthew 11:28

. . . .

Jesus, Lover and Shepherd of my soul, you promise rest to those who will come unto you, confessing weakness and weariness, and laying every burden down for you to bear. It is a rest that affects the physical body, but is deeper, too. You promise spiritual, soul rest to those who will come.

But sometimes I find that coming unto you is not my first response to the burdens I face. Sometimes I try even harder. I labor with even more effort, only to become even wearier than I was before. This is especially true when I face your law. I want so badly to be able to say, "I have done it. I am obedient. I am worthy."

Maybe coming unto you is so difficult because it means admitting that I am unable to meet the demands of the law.

It means that I am weak and that I am needy. I *can't* do it after all, regardless of how hard I try. To rest, I must confess that deep in my heart I am rest*less*. Your gracious call to me is for me to freely admit that the burden of the law and of life is far too weighty for me to carry.

Father, I thank you for showing me, even though the lessons have been painful, that it is only when I realize my inability to carry the load that I can experience rest. For your words to the apostle Paul are words that the Spirit is speaking to me: "*My grace* is sufficient for you, for *my power* is made perfect in weakness." The response of my heart echoes the apostle, saying, "Therefore, I will boast all the more gladly of my weaknesses so that *the power of Christ* may rest on me... for *when I am weak, then I am strong.*" How counterintuitive is that reasoning? How the logic of the gospel turns conventional, human wisdom upside down!

Yet my flesh is averse to confessing weakness. The result is that I live with a weary spirit and a burdened heart. How desperate I am for spiritual rest! Help me to listen and to learn. Your word tells me to "be strong in the Lord." *In the Lord.* Yes, that is the key for resting and being renewed with spiritual strength. For it is in resting that I am renewed, being renewed, empowered by your Spirit.

What would it be like to rest like this? To *really* rest. Maybe I need to start with physical rest? Maybe I need to take seriously your instruction to enjoy a sabbath. Maybe I need to learn how to call it a day, put my feet up, enjoy some tea, take a nap, and then throw the ball with my son. Maybe taking a break from vocational work will teach me that you, Jesus, have worked for me—that I must live by your *saving* and *sustaining* grace. That is the lesson of the Sabbath, isn't it? In teaching the Israelites their need for physical rest, you were providing a powerful analogy for their, and my, need for spiritual rest. You were the provider of the manna in the wilderness, and the provider of the Manna in the gospel.

This day, Jesus, my prayer is that I would hear your call to come unto you as my sovereign and saving God, confessing my weary and burdened heart, and then experiencing rest as I have never known. That I would so relax my soul in your grace and love, that the rest of the gospel would fill my heart—a rest that permeates—*utterly saturates*—my soul with your peace. So that when I speak, it may be rested speech... when I walk, it may be unhurried... when I pray, it may be empty of duty and guilt, and full of intimacy, peace and joy. Jesus, for your glory, teach me to rest.

Blessing the Lord

"I will bless the LORD at all times; his praise shall continually be in my mouth. My soul makes it boast in the LORD; let the humble hear and be glad."

Psalm 34:1-2 (ESV)

. . . .

Father in Heaven, I will bless your name because you have so richly blessed me. Your word tells me that you have provided me with "every spiritual blessing in Christ." Predestination. Regeneration. Propitiation. Expiation. Justification. Adoption. I am no longer condemned but set free in the Son. The list of spiritual blessings goes on and on and on, and every one is pure grace.

I confess my unworthiness to serve as a recipient of your lavish grace. But then, Father, I suppose that the only one who qualifies for grace is the one who does not deserve it, and that you have chosen to glorify yourself by sending your Son to rescue such a sinner as I from the consequences of my sin.

Even if there had never been the cross, creation would be enough to reveal your majesty and worthiness of receiving blessing and praise from all those whom you have made. Indeed, the splendor of the earth, the sea and the skies—the works of your hands—reveals your glory.

Yet, your greatest work was accomplished in Jesus, whose hands willingly received the nails in order that he might serve as the great substitute for sinners. Lord Jesus, how your praise should continually be in my heart and overflow from my lips. In worship. In conversation. In prayer.

However, Jesus, you know that your praise is not always in my mouth, and that the cause is a heart that grows cold to the glorious grace of your gospel. Rather than boasting in the cross and in who you are as my Savior King, I find that my sinful nature longs to boast in and extol itself. Not that I have anything to boast about. It just desires to boast in self, craving the opportunity to be praised and honored and appreciated. How heinous is this corruption of the soul, and how it grieves me to recognize this sin that resides so deeply in my flesh!

Holy Spirit, I pray for a genuine humility that is able to hear the good news that proclaims that my Jesus, the Good Shepherd, laid his life down for a sheep like me. A sheep that, as another pastor says, is far more sinful than he can freely admit, but now, because of his substitute Shepherd, is more forgiven, loved and accepted than he could ever dare to dream.

Spirit of God, help me to hear and believe the words of the gospel. Help me embrace that truth that "God shows his love for me in that while I was a sinner, Christ died for me... In this is love, not that I loved God, but that he loved me and sent his Son to be the propitiation for my sins... He himself bore my sins in his body on the tree, that I might die to sin and live to righteousness. By his wounds I have been healed."

Let me be one of the humble. One of the loved and healed. Let me be glad to be a saved sinner so that my heart will overflow again with spontaneous praise to you, my Father and giver of every spiritual blessing in the Savior. Enable me to believe the gospel so that I might die this day to sin and live unto righteousness as I bless the Lord who saves me and sustains me by his grace.

The Fullness of Joy

"In your presence there is fullness of joy; at your right hand are pleasures forevermore."

Psalm 16:11b (ESV)

· · · · · · · · ●●●●●● · · · · · · · · · · · ·

Abba, Father, how I want to experience the fullness of joy. Sometimes, I would settle for even a *taste* of joy. Like a starving sailor on a long journey who begins to forget the aroma of a home-cooked meal, I wonder if I have lost a sense of how true joy would feel. There are times when I think I've tasted it. Maybe what I've considered to be joy is merely the absence of pain or loss, when rich, deep, lasting joy is not gained from the elimination of negative circumstances, but from the manifest presence of God.

I suppose this is how so many people have been able to endure hardships, trials and persecutions. Considering your people in third world countries who have so little regarding material possessions, it seems that, while apparently a people to be pitied, they actually possess a quantity and quality of joy that I have never known. Maybe *I* am the one *they* pity.

When Peter spoke to a persecuted people in the first century, he said that the reason they were experiencing an "inexpressible joy" was because they fiercely believed the gospel and genuinely loved Jesus. They had their hope set on "an inheritance that is imperishable, undefiled and unfading, kept in heaven for you, who by God's power are being guarded through faith for a salvation ready to be revealed in the last time. In this you rejoice, though... you have been grieved by many trials."

That is what I need—your power to guard my heart from unbelief and to cultivate in me a longing for heaven and a love for Jesus, whose presence is all the inheritance I desire. For it is the presence of Jesus, by his indwelling Holy Spirit, that produces the fruit of joy. It is the presence of the One who died so that I might live. The One who was condemned so that I might be justified. The One who was forsaken so that I might become a son.

Oh, how the glory of your grace awakens my heart with a desire to follow and to honor you! How I want to know the sweetness of your presence, and abide there, in the compelling power of the gospel. Then I will be enabled to endure hardship and trials, knowing that through the cross I am a forgiven, beloved son, in whom and for whom you are working all things for my good and joy, and, and ultimately, for your glory. For I am learning that you are glorified when I live by faith and find my heart at rest in who you are for me as my God and Savior.

Father, as you guard my heart and strengthen my love for Jesus, would you give me the grace to repent of my heart's love for lesser joys? It grieves me to confess the broken cisterns from which I drink trying to find satisfaction for my soul. My flesh gives lip service to the joy of your presence, but in reality, seeks its joy in material possessions, physical comforts, worldly security and reputation.

In light of your promise of true joy in the gospel and by the grace of your Holy Spirit, I let go of and abandon my lesser joys, and embrace the hope of the present and eternal joy that is discovered by abiding in Jesus as my only righteousness. Maybe then I will experience a third-world joy, the kind of joy that says with the Psalmist, "There is nothing on earth that I desire besides you."

Rejecting the Lies

"But the serpent said to the woman,
'You will not surely die."

Genesis 3:4

· · · · · · · · ● ● ● ● ● ● ● ● · · · · · · ·

My faithful Father and God of truth, how I think upon the bait offered to Adam and Eve. It was a lie sugarcoated with a promise. Maybe in the instant they bit into the fruit and hit the hook they knew. Like a fish caught on a line, moments from death, I wonder how they fought the inevitable feeling. They had been deceived. They had been promised life and glory. But now they knew that the unavoidable consequence would befall them. Shame and death.

Why do I think that the consequences of biting into lies today are any different? Death, while ultimately physical, comes in many forms: the death of a friendship or a marriage; the death of integrity; the death of trust; the death of dreams. But the death that Adam and Eve experienced most immediately and acutely was not physical death. It was spiritual. No longer did they walk with you in freedom in the cool of the day. Now, with a sense of their moral corruption, they ran and hid from you in fear because of their guilt. That is the death that I know so well in my own life.

As an overflow of your steadfast love and as a fulfillment of your eternal purposes of grace, you made a promise to Adam and Eve. It is a promise for all your people—for each one who has, like them, bought the lie and taken the bite. In speaking to the serpent, you promised that there would be a descendent of the woman who would crush him and undo the curse. And your word tells us that Jesus is that descendant.

Lord Jesus, you fulfilled the original covenant that my first ancestors broke. They were tempted in the lush garden and failed. You were tested in the barren wilderness and were found faithful. You obeyed the Father in every detail, from external actions to internal desires and motivations. Though the enemy lied and used the bait of easy glory apart from the humiliation of the cross, you believed the word of the Father, saying that man does not live on bread alone but on every word that proceeds from the mouth of God.

There are times when I have thought, "If only I were in

the garden that day, I would not have taken the bait. I would have been faithful." But you know, Father, as do I in my saner moments, that I would have bought the lie, too. My own heart craves what the serpent offered to Adam and Eve—they wanted the glory of God for themselves. In fact, Father, isn't that what corrupted Satan? Didn't he grow jealous and desire to be worshipped as you are worshipped?

Isn't that what happens in my own heart when I live according to my flesh rather than by your Spirit? How loathsome that sin is, that act of ultimate treason. Longing for the praise and worship of men—the praise that only you deserve and should receive. How I pray today that I would be given the grace to crucify my flesh anew through repentance so that I may have a fresh love for the Savior, and a consuming passion to see him exalted.

May I find my joy today in your glory—the glory revealed in the truth of the gospel, which tells me that though Satan has deceived, Jesus has saved. Yes, in Jesus there is truth (I deserve condemnation) and grace (Jesus was condemned for me). In light of that amazing mercy and by the power of your indwelling Holy Spirit, enable me to reject the lies of the evil one, and to live by the truth and grace of God. Father, for your glory, it is to that end that I pray.

Drawing Near

"Let us with confidence draw near to the throne of grace,
that we may receive mercy and find grace
to help in time of need."

Hebrews 4:16 (ESV)

· · · · · · ● ● ● ● ● ● ● ● ● ● ● · · · · · · ·

Sovereign Father, how I thank you that I have a great high priest in Jesus—a Savior who was tempted and tested in every way but proved utterly faithful to you as a Son. He now stands as my representative, my high priest in heaven, imputing his righteousness to me and making me beautiful in your sight. I, too, am now counted as a son, and invited to the throne in my time of need.

Why then is it that I so infrequently draw near to you? Why I do neglect the abundant supply of your mercy? Rather than approach your throne of grace, why do I busy myself with worry and worldly schemes? Why is prayer a last resort, if I even resort to it at all? Shouldn't drawing near in prayer be my first response to every circumstance and need that I face?

Father, I confess my unbelief. Regrettably, I live much of my life in atheistic self-sufficiency, and must live with the consequences of worry, stress, outbursts of anger, pride, selfishness, depression, fear, anxiety, and the like. But your word tells me to cast my anxieties, and every other weed of unbelief, on you, for you care for me. As a father loves his child, so you love me. And you are a sovereign Father, who orders all events and circumstances in such a way that all things ultimately work for the good—*the blessing*—of those who love you and have been called by you to be adopted and dearly loved sons and daughters.

Yet I think another reason why I do not draw near is another symptom of unbelief—*guilt.* It is just so hard for me to believe that my sin has been atoned, covered, and cleansed by the blood of Jesus. Yet, as John said, if I confess my sins, you are faithful and just to forgive and to cleanse every stain.

I want to believe and rest in the fact that, because of the cross, I am now invited to draw near to your throne. Not the throne of *judgment*, but the throne of *grace*, so that I may receive help from the omnipotent God who has invited me to call him Abba.

My Abba, what I need today is grace. Grace upon grace to repent, believe and live in the context of your sovereign care and abounding resources of mercy. Help me to draw near, not long after my time of need, but during my time of need. Help me bring all my cares, whether cares of anxiety or guilt, before you.

Father, enable me to abide in the truth of Charitie Lees Bancroft's hymn that says,

> *Before the throne of God above, I have a strong and perfect plea; a great High Priest whose name is Love who ever lives and pleads for me.*
>
> *When Satan tempts me to despair and tells me of the guilt within; Upward I look and see Him there, Who made an end to all my sin.*
>
> *Because the sinless Savior died my sinful soul is counted free; For God the Just is satisfied to look on Him and pardon me.*

Yes, Lord, I believe. Help my unbelief so that I may draw near and find grace and mercy in my time of need.

The Kindness of God

"So, Mephibosheth ate at David's table,
like one of the king's sons."

2 Samuel 9:11

· · · · · · · · ●●●●●●●●●● · · · · · · · ·

Great God of abundant grace, you know that I love the story of David and Mephibosheth. As the grandson of the former king, Saul, and son of Jonathan, he was a potential rival to the king's throne. Any other monarch would have had him found out and eliminated. That scenario would be expected. In fact, Mephibosheth expected it himself. Living in a desolate part of the kingdom, he hoped never to be discovered. The former member of the royal family was now living in poverty on Lo-debar, the city of no promise.

Yet David's desire was not to eliminate his enemy, but rather to show kindness to anyone left in the house of Saul, for the sake of his best friend, Jonathan. He called it the kindness of God. When I look at David's heart toward

Mephibosheth, I am struck how much it parallels your heart toward me.

He was born into royalty and then experienced a fall that left him lame in both feet. He was no real rival to the king. He certainly had nothing to offer by way of practical service. Mephibosheth could not fight in the army or even serve a cup of tea. He was a weak, helpless man, with many fears, insecurities, and needs. Then David sought him out, not to curse or judge, but to *bless*.

Father, I am Mephibosheth. I, too, am lame. Not in my feet, but in my flesh. Apart from your Spirit, I am unable to take even one step spiritually. Yet you sought me out, not to curse or judge, but to bless—and bless beyond my wildest imagination.

Just as David supplied Mephibosheth with thirty-six servants with seventy-two feet to serve him by meeting his needs, you have supplied me with the life-giving ministry of Jesus. Father, he worked for my salvation, securing my justification and giving me the Spirit to enable my sanctification. Every spiritual blessing I have is the result of Jesus serving and blessing a moral and spiritual cripple like me.

Thank you, Jesus! Thank you for humbling yourself to death, even death on a cross, where your feet were nailed, and you became a cripple in my place. As my substitute, you paid the cost for my adoption so that I, like

Mephibosheth, might be invited to eat at the King's table of grace, being sustained not merely on that which is physical and temporal, but sustained by that which is spiritual and eternal—the bread of life and the cup of salvation.

May I believe today that I can come into your presence as a son and, lame as I am, be given the grace to walk in your ways by the indwelling power of your Holy Spirit. I desire the ability to step out in faith and follow where you lead. As a recipient of abundant, overwhelming grace, I want to walk in line with the gospel. I want to repent. I want to believe and to experience the fruit of the Spirit. But I know that if I am to live as if I can walk, it will be because I am being carried, like Mephibosheth. Carried by the enabling grace of your Spirit, who gives feet to the lame and the place of a son at the table of the King.

Walking by the Spirit

*"But I say, walk by the Sprit, and you will not
gratify the desires of the flesh."*

Galatians 5:16 (ESV)

· · · · · · · · · ● ● ● ● ● ● ● · · · · · · · ·

My God of grace, you know the battle that is waged
every day in my mind and in my heart. My flesh desires that
which is contrary to the Spirit and your Word. Whether it
is the worldly sin of the younger brother or the religious,
self-righteous sin of the elder brother, my sinful nature
continues to lie, tempt, and deceive. Repentantly, I confess
that that far too often I have gratified the desires of that
rebellious, insidiously evil nature.

Nevertheless, I am thankful that there is a battle being
fought. Father, apart from the Spirit's work in my life, I
would not even struggle with sin. It would utterly rule me.
And still, sometimes I do not put up much of a fight against
it. I think that it is so easy at times to give in and succumb,

because too often I do not live in view of the cross or in fellowship with the Spirit. But by your grace, Holy Spirit, you prick my conscience and convict me of my personal betrayal. Yes, my sin is not merely breaking a law. It is not merely legal, it is also relational and personal, and is a blatant betrayal of Jesus as my Savior, Lord, and Treasure.

Father, I suppose that is why you are discipling me to "walk by the Spirit" and not merely to try harder to keep the law. You know that I, even with a new heart, do not have the capacity to resist the pull of sin that still resides in my earthly nature. You have given me a new heart, so that I will have new eyes to see my need for Jesus and the Holy Spirit. The law drives me to Jesus and Jesus gives me the Spirit, whose indwelling power and influence is exponentially greater than the strength of my flesh. That is why Paul said that if I walk by the Spirit, I will not gratify the desires of the flesh, but rather I will manifest the fruit of the Spirit—fruit that only the Spirit can produce.

Your Word teaches me that the key to walking by the Spirit is to live by faith in the redemptive work of Jesus, whose word has taught me that the Spirit flows with power in my life when I abide in his righteousness. Jesus, you are the vine, and I am merely a branch. Apart from you and your indwelling Spirit I can do nothing.

Now, the call to my heart is to die to sin—to crucify it through repentance—and rest in the atoning, reconciling work of the cross. It is through living by faith in the gospel that I am empowered to live a life filled with the presence and power of the Spirit.

I pray today for the grace to believe that I am complete in the gift that you have given to me in the gospel. Through faith in the substitutionary work of Jesus, I have been forgiven and declared righteous. I am a son of the King. The Spirit of God dwells in me.

O Father, help my mind and heart to be gripped with the joy of knowing you as my Treasure and abiding in your presence, so that when the substitute joys that my flesh craves begin to tempt my soul, not only will I walk away from my sin, but I will also walk to Jesus, so that I may place my weak hand into his. It is then that I will experience what it means to walk by the Spirit, living in his power and manifesting his fruit.

Assurance of Grace

"I am sure of this, that he who began a good work in you
will bring it to completion at the day
of Jesus Christ."

Philippians 1:6

. . . . ● ● ● ● ● ● ● ● ● ● . . . .

Father, I am thankful for these words of Paul, words that are meant to encourage and build up in the presence of potentially discouraging circumstances. They remind me that the doctrine of the perseverance of the saints, while true and important, is ultimately eclipsed by the doctrine of the preservation of the saints by God, which is also true and vitally important. I need to remember every day that my salvation is not ultimately dependent upon *my grip* on you, but upon *your grip* on me.

For as the hymn writer penned, I am "prone to wander, Lord I feel it, prone to leave the God I love." If the mortgage of my eternal home were to depend upon the degree of my sanctification, I am certain that you would foreclose, and I would be a homeless man again. But the gospel tells me that the price has been paid in full with the blood of the Savior.

As Revelation says, you "purchased men for God." You have not left me as an orphan but have sent the Holy Spirit into my heart to cry out "Abba, Father." In fact, Jesus, you have promised that you are preparing an eternal home in which I will dwell forever. It is a dwelling of mercy, built and paid for by grace alone.

Yet I still doubt. It is so difficult to believe that I have been completely forgiven—past, present and future—and fully reconciled to you as my God and Father. There is a voice in my heart that continues to condemn. I know that is not of your Spirit, but it is the rebellious flesh, refusing to let me live in the liberty and peace of the gospel.

For some reason, I believe that voice. While I can be so sure of your grace toward others, I am not always so sure for myself. Maybe that is because I am more intimately aware of my own sin and unworthiness than I am of theirs. Whatever the reason, I confess a failure to trust that the work you have begun in my life will result in complete salvation in the last day.

My prayer today is to believe, with a humble, yet confident assurance of your grace, that you will not let me go. That Jesus, as you said, "My sheep hear my voice and I know them, and they follow me. I give them eternal life, and they will never perish, and no one will snatch them out of my hand." As a sheep, I do not follow as well as I desire to follow. But I do desire to follow you, and to reject the lies of the flesh and of the evil one.

You began the work of grace in my heart and you will complete it. I will stand in your presence one day as a righteous son, delighting in you my God, knowing perfectly the promise of the gospel that "there is no condemnation for those who are in Christ Jesus."

No More Tears

"He will wipe away every tear from their eyes, and death shall be no more, neither shall there be mourning nor crying nor pain anymore, for the former things have passed away. And he who was seated on the throne said, 'Behold! I am making all things new!'"

Revelation 21:4-5a (ESV)

· · · · · · · · · · · · ● · · · · · · · · · · · ·

My Father in Heaven, how I long for the day when there will be no more tears, no more death, no more sadness or crying or pain. Since Adam and Eve initiated the curse, there has not been a day that the consequences of sin have not been felt. Relational brokenness. Violence. Theft. Lying. Murder. Self-righteousness. Bigotry. And the earth has not been unaffected. Storms, earthquakes, floods and the like have caused unceasing grief among humanity.

I thank you, my compassionate Savior, that you are well acquainted with my tears. Some flow as the result of my own foolish, and often sinful, choices. Others stain my face because of the curse on the earth. Sickness and death have separated me from those whom I love. The wounds of betrayers and enemies have produced their own share of tears. I have been the object of affliction from other evil men.

Yet, Jesus, you know the effects of the fall more intimately than anyone. As the Man of Sorrows, you are well familiar with the depths of human grief, none of which was due to your fault or neglect. Not only did you suffer in the flesh from unjust accusation, betrayal and ultimately a brutal death, but your soul also bore the full weight of the justice for the sins of your people (including mine), as you experienced the spiritual agony of God's righteous judgment on the cross.

The cross teaches me that as my substitute, you redeemed me from the curse of the law by becoming a curse for me. Therefore, I will not weep in judgment. When this life passes, and you initiate the age of consummation, I will live in paradise. No more tears, sadness, crying or pain. Nothing but undiluted, perfect, and inexpressible joy in your presence. As Paul said, "I consider the sufferings of this present time are not worth comparing to the glory that is to be revealed to us." For many, the suffering is severe. So, I trust that the glory you will reveal to your people is utterly beyond our finite human comprehension. What an encouragement that is to my heart, Father.

What would it be like for me to live with that hope now? What if I could anchor my heart today to the reality of eternal joy? What might that kind of faith enable me to endure? Honestly, Father, I don't want to find out. I do not desire the kinds of trials that you speak of in your word that prove the refining fire to faith.

But I have tasted the fire, and know that more trials, even more severe than I have yet known, will come. So, prepare my mind and heart now to face the sorrow and the sadness then. May I grieve fully as a human, but not without the hope that has been promised to me in the gospel.

My prayer today is that you would grant me a full supply of sustaining grace and a faith that is overflowing with hope. When I taste the saltiness of tears, may I be reminded of your sweetness, knowing that sorrows in this life serve joy as the law serves the gospel, which drives me to Jesus with every command.

The Idolatry of Reputation

"They do all their deeds to be seen by others."
Matthew 23:5a (ESV)

. . . . ●●●●●●●●●●● . . . .

Lord Jesus, when you warned your disciples about having a Pharisaical heart, you were warning them of replacing the gift of the gospel with the beauty of one's reputation as the prize of the heart. The Pharisee, as a member of a respected group within Judaism, lived for the praise of men. If he prayed, he wanted people to hear his eloquence. If he gave, he made sure that others saw the greatness of his generosity. Any "righteous deed" done was "to be seen by others." For the Pharisee, righteousness was not something to be received as a grace-gift, it was a reputation that was earned, sustained and ultimately defined by his moral standing in the eyes of his peers.

Sadly, as I reflect upon my heart, your indictment upon

the Pharisees is one that exposes my own motives. I confess that the driving factor that motivates my public deeds is rarely love for you or my neighbor, but rather how my actions or words will reflect upon me. I, too, live for the praise of men, and am becoming more and more aware of how little I actually rest in the gospel—the gospel that provides me with my true reputation as an unworthy sinner who was loved and adopted by a King. It is a reputation that dies to the perceptions of the world and boasts only in the cross. It is a reputation that thinks little about itself, but so much about the fame, honor and glory of Jesus.

In light of the gospel, it is my desire today to have your Holy Spirit fill me and consume my heart in such a way that I am enabled to truly and deeply repent of my pursuit of self-glory. As an adopted son, may I recognize the spirit of fear that wants me to be consumed with the opinions of the world. By the power of your Sprit, may I not live in response to what others think or say, nor out of duty or mere social expectation. But may I live with a quiet confidence that my reputation in heaven is that of a righteous, beloved son.

Thank you, Jesus. Oh, thank you, Jesus, for giving me an imputed righteousness that now serves as the basis for my heavenly reputation, which by the power of your grace is able to heal emotional wounds, mend insecurities and provide the gospel power that I need to break from the idolatry of a worldly reputation.

Like a car with its wheels out of alignment, my heart will continually pull me toward the pursuit of that worldly reputation. When I succeed, I get proud. When I fail, I get depressed. Father, let both pride and depression, including their cousins, anger, fear, gossip, and insecurity, be red flags concerning this misalignment in my heart. Enable me in that moment of awareness to realign my mind with the truth of the gospel, so that it can speak the truth of grace to my heart. Then, as I am preaching the gospel to myself, enable me to believe who I am in Jesus, and to celebrate and worship him, boasting along with Paul, "only in the cross of Christ Jesus my Lord."

Let me define my life not by what the world tells me I am, but by what you tell me I am. Then I will be free to love. No more mere duty or sheer obligation. I will be free to follow Jesus and be used as an instrument of his love in the lives of others, as the counter-cultural life of radical grace transforms a recovering Pharisee into a believing son.

New Mercies

"The steadfast love of the Lord never ceases; his mercies never come to an end; they are new every morning; great is your faithfulness. The LORD is my portion, says my soul, therefore I will hope in him."

Lamentations 3:22-24

. . . .

My merciful Father, even amid tragedy and heartbreak, Jeremiah was able to affirm the steadfastness of your covenant faithfulness and love. Although he could not understand the mysteries of your providence, he still held fast to the mercies that are new for your people every day. You have promised to work all things for good for those who love you and who have been called to participate in the fulfillment of your redemptive purposes, even when those purposes cause my heart to question my mind's understanding of your sovereignty, goodness and wisdom.

David prayed, "Even though I walk through the valley of the shadow of death, I will fear no evil, for you are with me." There will be evil. Sin will appear to have won the day. However, just as you were with David, Daniel, Meshach, Shadrach and Abednego, Paul, Peter and others, so you are also with me. Though I walk through the fire, I will not be burned, for Jesus was burned in my place. He experienced the separation, the forsakenness, and the judgement that I will never have to know. You are with me as a Shepherd and a Father. Even in the valley of the shadow of death.

Like Jeremiah, I am called to confess my shortsightedness and put my trust and hope in your sovereign, good, wise and perfect will. Yet as a man who far too often lives by the flesh rather than by the Spirit, this is no easy task. For in its finite arrogance, my sin nature believes that I would be a better captain of my life and of your world. As a result, I awake each morning with a multitude of concerns, fears, and worries. Rather than meet with you and put my hope in you as my Sovereign Father, I tend to bypass my only real source of peace, strength and rest, launching into the day ill-equipped with the weakness of my own ability.

Today it is my desire to avoid the bypass.

I want to meet you in the morning and experience afresh the newness of your mercies, the steadfast love, covenant faithfulness and abundant grace that is available to those who believe. I want to embrace the gift of a Savior, knowing that I have been given every spiritual blessing in him. Even though I pass through the fire and feel its heat, you have promised that I will not be burned. Judgement has been fulfilled in the cross. Life is now to be lived in a faith union with Jesus.

Therefore, I am to believe today, and tomorrow, and the next day. Anew. Because your mercies are new and are to be embraced every morning. Your grace never grows dull or loses its power. It is available. If only I will believe.

So, I come to you, to the God who has covered my sins with the blood of his Son. To my Father who is more willing to forgive than I am to repent, I come to claim your mercies and abide in your grace today, praying with Jeremiah, "The Lord is my portion, says my soul, therefore I will hope in him."

It is Finished

"It is finished!"

John 19:30

· · · · · · · ● · ● ● ● ● ● ● ● ● ● · ● · · · · · · ·

Abba, Father, when Jesus spoke those words on the cross, he intended for them to echo throughout time, that each new generation, by the enabling grace of your Holy Spirit, would hear and believe the good news. My mind and my heart worship you with thanksgiving, considering your eternal mercy that opened *my* ears and gave *me* eyes to see my own need for such a great salvation as expressed in the cry "It is finished!"

Those three words contain the promise that the law has been fulfilled. Lord Jesus, as you said in the Sermon on the Mount, you did not come to abolish the law and reduce the demand for perfect obedience; you came to accomplish the complete keeping of those demands. You did not only *die* for me as a substitute. You also *lived* for me as a substitute. When I consider that angle on your grace, I begin to understand a bit better what John Newton meant when he wrote the lines: "To see the law by Christ fulfilled, to hear his pardoning voice, turns a slave into a child, and duty into choice."

Because of your life lived for me, Jesus, the curse of the law's demands has been broken. The shackles have been loosed and I am free. Free to live and love and repent and believe and forgive as I abide in your finished work on my behalf. For you not only fulfilled the law, you were the one who was shackled—nailed—to the cross in order that the justice my sins required might also be fulfilled. There is no more fear or possibility of accusation. As your word says, "Who shall bring any charge against God's elect? It is God who justifies." Who shall bring *any* charge! Father, because of the propitiation of Jesus' blood, there is not one sin that can be brought up against me. You will throw out all charges since they have been nailed to the cross.

What glorious grace!

Yet I live as if the law had not been fulfilled. And in so doing, I deny your grace. I forsake the gospel. When my sin is revealed, rather than running to you for mercy and claiming the atoning blood of Jesus, I wallow in self-pity. Sometimes I try to justify myself, or shift blame to someone else. On other occasions I try to do penance and atone myself, making promises that I think somehow will offset the guilt.

Father, I give my flesh and its sin too much power in my life. The *gospel* is the power of God. The cross and the Spirit is what I need when faced with my abiding propensity toward iniquity. I need to gaze upon my Jesus saying, "It... is... *finished!*" Sins past. Sins present. Sins future. The law keeping is done. The law-breaking is forgiven. Forever. It is finished. I have been set free. So, don't go back to the slavery of the law. It is for freedom that Christ has set me free.

As a gift of grace, when I am tempted to live like a Pharisee and gaze at myself, would you enable me to fix my eyes on Jesus, who for the joy set before him endured the cross for me? Would you realign my heart to that of a child who lives in full faith-dependence upon his Abba? Would you this day enable me to fully embrace the depth of my sin, but at the same time, to fully embrace the depth, height, breadth and width of the finished work of Jesus, whose grace is far greater than my sin?

Abba, Father, by the power of your Spirit, enable me to believe that it *is* finished, so that I can begin to really live in the freedom of the gospel.

Grace Flows Downhill

"Clothe yourselves, all of you, with humility toward one another, for God opposes the proud but gives grace to the humble."
1 Peter 5:5b

· · · · · · · · · · · · ● · · · · · · · · · · · · ·

My God and my King, how beautiful is humility. How glorious is the scene of my Savior emptying himself of divine rights and privileges, taking on flesh and sacrificing himself as a substitute for sinners like me on a cross. It is the ultimate expression of humility. The conscious, volitional, purposeful lowering of himself to serve and bless. To wash dirty feet. To hang and bleed. To suffer and save.

Humility is beautiful and glorious. It is also *powerful*. When my mind and heart begin to absorb the implications of the price of my redemption, my knees give way and my hands rise in worship. Jesus, the humility you displayed in my salvation motivates me with a deep, spiritual urge to experience the emptying of self for the sake of another.

Yet, like putting on a shirt that is way too small and that I cannot pull over my head, humility does not seem to fit my heart. Father, I realize that it is because my flesh is so big-headed and proud. Even my insecurities are, at the root, expressions of self-glory. Wanting to be someone and having a name. Desiring the praise of men. Demanding rights. Gossiping out of jealousy. Scheming a way to get noticed and recognized. Worrying about what people think about me.

Abba, my proud heart repulses me—*especially the insecurities*. I can identify with Paul when he cried out, "Who will save me from this body of death?" And then, as if pulling all his mental faculties together, he finds the cross. "Thanks be to God through Jesus Christ our Lord... there is therefore now no condemnation for those who are in Christ Jesus!" That is what I need. Yes, apart from Jesus and the sweet aroma of the gospel, I am just a rotting corpse. But you have delivered me from myself. In the gospel, you have declared me to legally righteous and personally loved.

Yes, grace flows downhill. You give grace to the humble. To those who know they are proud and hate it. To those who know they don't measure up and, in their weakness, cry out for mercy. Grace is given to the publican who looks for a substitute, not the Pharisee who is pleased with himself. As David experienced in his own brokenness, "A broken and contrite heart, O God, you will not despise."

So, let me wear the robe of humility. Shape my heart so that it will fit and so that I will gladly adorn a lesser concern for self and ever-increasing delight in the cross. Teach me to wash feet. How to love and forgive and listen. Teach me how to die so that I might live.

As I die to self-righteousness and self-importance and self-concern, will you show me my heart, that I may be humbled? But as you humble me by revealing my sin and need, will you give me the faith to look to Jesus and to believe that he is the propitiation for my sins? There is no more justice to serve. No more wrath to endure. The price is paid. Grace flows downhill. Oh, may I remember this!

May I live in that place of need and of grace, knowing that one day you will lift me up, as you did Jesus. Yes, you have promised that grace will lead to glorification, and to the eternal and perfect praise of the One whose name is above every name. You are my humble and glorious savior, Jesus.

Forgiveness

"As the Lord has forgiven you, so you also must forgive."

Colossians 3:13b (ESV)

· · · · · · ● ● ● ● ● ● ● ● ● ● ● ● · · · · · ·

My God and Cleanser of my soul, I thank you for forgiving me of my sins by nailing them to the cross, "canceling the record of debt that stood against me with its legal demands." As Corrie ten Boom said, you have cast them into the depth of the sea and promised never to bring them up against me again. For that is what forgiveness is: *paying a debt and never mentioning it against someone again.* Forgiveness is an act of grace, and it has freely flown down upon me like a flooding river of blessing to water the soil of my heart; that it may bring life and freedom. As your word encourages me, "There is now no condemnation for those who are in Christ Jesus."

Yet I am so aware of my propensity to be hard-hearted and unforgiving. Being one who is not condemned, I so easily condemn. Being so richly forgiven, I am so slow to forgive. Having the floodgates of grace opened to me, I tend to build dams that restrict the flow to others. My flesh is quick to inflict justice, but so stubbornly resistant to release mercy.

I realize that this is not consistent with how you have treated me, and I fear that I have taken your grace for granted, considering my own forgiveness an entitlement. Maybe my refusal to forgive, but to grow bitter and resentful, is why my heart becomes so stagnant and lifeless. And when that happens in my heart, I become cold and indifferent even to you.

I know it is true and I despise the condition, for in your kindness you have shown me that forgiveness is not merely a legal transaction, but is the entryway into a grace-oriented, love-saturated relationship. In Jesus, you have taken away my sin so that I may know and enjoy you, without the fear of the law's legal demands which Jesus fulfilled on my behalf. No, forgiveness does not merely displace me from penalty, it draws me into your embrace, like the younger brother to his love-sick father, so that I may know that I am accepted... *and have been missed*. And so, when I do not forgive, my own spiritual health suffers.

In view of your great mercy to me, I desire to forgive.

But let it begin with my own forgiveness. May I begin again today in the gospel's promise that I am forgiven, and that with the blood of Jesus over my life, my new sins are forgiven before I even repent. Blessed is the man whose transgressions the Lord does not count against him.

Father, I am such a blessed man!

As I am learning, forgiveness is an implication of the gospel and an *overflow* of *grace*. So may your act of grace toward me in the Savior be the fuel that empowers me to forgive others from my heart, and not merely out of obligation. May your forgiving love and grace overflow in my heart with a flood-tide desire to extend debt-paying, throw-it-into-the-sea, genuinely reconciling forgiveness to my debtors. I trust that the result will be not only a blessing to the one forgiven, but an unexpected joy in my own heart, as one who is learning to break the dam, release the grace, and have the resurrection life of Jesus lived through me.

Working All Things for Good

"As for you, you meant evil against me, but God meant it for good, to bring it about that many people should be kept alive, as they are today."

Genesis 50:20 (ESV)

· · · · · · · · · · · · ● ● ● ● ● ● · · · · · · · · ·

Sovereign Father, how I pray that you would enable me to see the events of my life the way that Joseph was able to see his. The once favored son was sold into slavery, accused of a crime he did not commit, and placed in prison for thirteen years in the prime of his life. I'm afraid to consider how I would respond if I were in his shoes. So, I pray for eyes to see your hand in every event of my life—especially in the events that don't make sense to me now.

You know how I look back with regret and would go back and change so many decisions in my life if I were able. I wonder if Joseph ever sat on the cold floor of the dungeon with his head in his hands saying, "What if... what if... what if?" Father, I would know how he felt, since I, too, have thought on so many occasions, "If I could only go back and make that decision over." But I can't. I think what you are teaching me, and showing me in the life of Joseph, is that you are sovereign over every detail, even the apparently poor choices in my life that have brought me pain, sorrow, grief and regret.

What is more, you are not only sovereign over them, but have ordained them and are using them to accomplish a purpose in and through my life that I cannot, at this moment, discern. While imprisoned with little hope of release, Joseph could not have imagined that you would raise him up to be the savior of the known world, the manager of grain who would have the wisdom and ability to provide grain during a great famine. But it's true; many lives were spared through Joseph. And a huge part of that plan was his humiliation and suffering.

Lord Jesus, you can identify with Joseph on a much deeper level that I will ever be able to relate. You decided to come to this world and endure the ultimate pain, sorrow and grief by pursuing the cross. You experienced no regret. It was the plan—a plan that accomplished the saving of many lives, even mine.

The Pharisees, Sadducees, the crowds of Jews and Roman guards all intended your crucifixion for evil, but the

Father meant it for good. I suppose even the disciples experienced the "what if" on that sad weekend of Passover when you were thought to be dead. Weren't they depressed and wondering what they could have done to prevent such an evil event from taking place?

Then you rose and showed them and me in a glorious fashion, that our God works all things for good for those who love him and have been called according to his purpose. If the cross was part of your plan, then I can certainly see the much smaller crosses in my life as part of your design. Today, Father, I pray that I would have eyes to see your sovereignty, and faith to trust your perfect plan.

Inexpressible Joy

"Blessed be the God and Father of our Lord Jesus Christ! According to his great mercy, he has caused us to be born again to a living hope through the resurrection of Jesus Christ from the dead, to an inheritance that is imperishable, undefiled, and unfading, kept in heaven for you... Though you have not seen him, you love him. Though you do not now see him, you believe in him and rejoice with joy that is inexpressible and filled with glory."

1 Peter 1:3-4, 8

. . . .

Father, there is so much for my head and my heart to grasp and enjoy in these two verses. Yet I suppose it may be that the meat of these truths may never get broken down into sufficient bites for me to fully digest in this life. But how I want to abide in the reality of which they speak. New birth. Living hope. Resurrection. An imperishable inheritance. Heaven.

All the result of your great mercy!

But the one thing I want to focus on right now is heaven, since I find that it is so easy to want my heaven in the here and now. But you tell me that I, while enjoying an abundance of grace even now, must wait with a "living hope" for what lies ahead. So may hope live. May it thrive in my heart today.

You have taught me that the resurrection of Jesus is a guarantee of my own resurrection. Unless Jesus returns quickly, I will die. But by grace, having been born again, I have the hope of eternal glory and the "imperishable, undefiled and unfading inheritance." Can it really be true? I have an inheritance from the sovereign God? My Father, who created and owns the universe, has left me, one of his sons, an eternal gift? What could that be?

Father, I'm tempted, like the young prodigal, to ask for my portion now! However, I realize that it is an inheritance that is "kept in heaven." Father, I pray for the faith to have that hope, and a heart that *longs for heaven.*

But you have also taught me that the inheritance is not essentially stuff. It is not what my flesh wants now, but the craving that the Spirit is weaving into my heart—the longing not just for heaven, but for *him...* for Jesus. That I may see Jesus face to face. That I may worship him and enjoy him and adore him.

Your word tells me that to be in the presence of God,

face to face with my Savior, will be the *fullness* of joy. And I think that is what I really desire—the fullness of joy! The kind of joy that inspires the mind and inflames the heart. The kind of joy that Peter says is so deep, rich, and wonderful, that it is ultimately an *inexpressible* joy.

Like those to whom Peter wrote, I love Jesus because he loved me. And the desire of my heart is to experience his presence today in such a way that I, even on this side of eternity, can *taste* and *experience* that joy—the inexpressible joy of seeing, knowing, and savoring my sin-bearing, life-giving, and hope-imparting Jesus.

Abiding in the Vine

"Abide in me, and I will abide in you. As the branch cannot bear fruit by itself, unless it abides in the vine, neither can you, unless you abide in me. I am the vine; you are the branches. Whoever abides in me and I in him, he it is that bears much fruit, for apart from me you can do nothing."

John 15:4-5

. . . .

My generous Father, I thank you for your ingrafting grace. You took a dead branch like me and attached it to the vine of Jesus, so that I may draw my life from him. His righteousness is now mine, and the sap of the Holy Spirit now flows into me so that I may produce fruit. The glorious fruit of humble repentance and joyful faith. Of love, peace, patience, goodness, gentleness, and the rest.

Yet why do I so often fail to see those virtues on my

branch? What is my problem? According to Jesus, I fail to see fruit because I fail to *consciously abide* in him as my righteousness. Rather than finding my life in Jesus, I seek it in other things. Your word calls these Jesus-substitutes idols: Success. Reputation. Honors. Possessions.

If I am honest, I think that I try to find my life in my ministry as I seek to abide in the "praise of men." Sometimes I seek to abide in safety and comfort. Sometimes it is in a worldly pleasure that treasures the gift more than the giver. Whatever it is, I confess that my heart drifts after these idolatrous Jesus-substitutes. Father, that is why I need so desperately to consciously abide in Jesus anew, every day.

It is *then* that I will see fruit, the evidence of your Spirit, in my life. And may my motive for a fruit-filled life be your glory for taking a dead branch and making it live. As I live by gospel-faith and am empowered by your Spirit to love selflessly with joy and gladness, I pray that my life will be a blessing to others, particularly my family. May I experience joy and peace when circumstances mitigate against it, and may I know patience, kindness and gentleness, faithfulness, goodness and self-control, when my flesh would be inclined toward the opposite.

But above all fruit, I pray that I would experience the glory of humble repentance, along with joyful faith. To bring my sin without excuse to the cross and believe that my deadness has been forgiven and that new life has been imputed by the merits of my Savior. To glory in Jesus as my only and fully sufficient righteousness. That is what it means to abide. By grace, that is what I will do in this moment, and by more grace, in moments to come. *I will abide in Jesus.*

Living by Faith

"Trust in the LORD with all your heart,
and lean not on your understanding."

Proverbs 3:5

· · · · · · · · · ●●●●●● · · · · · · · · · · ·

My Savior Jesus, I confess that there is nothing more difficult for me than to live by faith. It's not because you are untrustworthy. As you know, my mind has no trouble affirming your sovereignty, and testifying to your goodness and wisdom. My head is on board. It is my heart that is so resistant. Yet here in Proverbs you tell me to trust you with all my heart, and not to lean on my own understanding.

When I realize this applies to the totality of my life, I am simply overwhelmed with my lack of faith. I am always leaning on my own understanding, and on my own ability to perform and to control my own life. I feverishly attempt to manage all contingencies, and as a result, live a life of worry rather than a life of faith. When I refuse to trust you, I trade in a spirit of sonship for the slavery of orphanhood, where I live in bondage to worry, insecurity and fear.

This plays itself out not only in the context of worry, but at the very heart of my relationship with you, Jesus. When I fail to trust you with my heart, I may profess to be saved by the grace of your substitutionary life, death and resurrection, but in reality I live as if I must perform in order to be loved and accepted. At least I feel as if I must perform to *maintain* the love, acceptance and righteousness that the gospel proclaims is now mine. And so, I become a practical Pharisee, basing my justification upon my sanctification. This does not glorify you, Jesus, since this kind of life depends on my ability rather than on your grace.

What am I to do? How can I change? Proverbs 3:5. Ah, yes. Trust in the LORD with *all* my heart. My Savior Jesus, I want that that kind of heart. I want to trust you as my wonderful justifying Savior, my merciful adopting Savior, and my powerful sanctifying Savior.

As I come to you today praying for that faith, I repent of the worry, insecurity and fear that reveals such a hard and proud heart. As an act of gospel-faith, I will put my trust in you.

Belonging to Jesus

"And you also are among those who are called to belong to Jesus Christ. To all in Rome who are loved by God and called to be saints."

Romans 1:6-7

. . . . ●●●●●● . . . .

Abba, Father, I remember playing kickball at recess in elementary school. You know how I always wanted to be a captain because I feared that I would otherwise be picked either in the middle of the group or near the bottom. I wanted to be wanted, not just tolerated.

Yet, Father, sometimes I feel that way as a Christian. I see so much of my lack of holiness and so much of my unworthiness, that I fear, while I am a son, I am one whom you only *tolerate*. My heart tells me that you put up with me because you must, not because you really want to. Day after day my sin rises like a flood and I begin to drown in guilt. My heart whispers, "Certainly, I am one of your last picks, and maybe… maybe you wish you had not chosen me at all."

But the opening words of Paul to the Romans pull me back. Even though my heart resists, you are calling out by your Spirit through the apostle, "You also… belong to Jesus." You tell me that I am not merely tolerated, but dearly "*loved.*" Can this really be true? I, who deserve to be kicked off the team daily, belong to Jesus because God loves me? Can this *really* be true? In that moment of uncertainty and questioning, I thank you, Holy Spirit, for continually revealing the cross of Christ to my heart, where the Father has demonstrated his love by purchasing me with the blood of Jesus. Even though I do not feel worthy, the gospel proclaims your acceptance and love, forgiveness, and grace.

What an amazing joy it is to realize that you have declared me, as an unworthy member of the kingdom, to be a *saint*, a "holy one." Not because I am holy, but because Jesus was holy for me. He is my substitute holiness, which is why he didn't just die for me but also lived for me. As your Word says, you died for and justify the *ungodly*! When I was to be rightfully condemned as a sinner, Christ died for me, and through receiving the gift of his work by faith, I am counted righteous, holy, a fully forgiven son. Not *tolerated* but *treasured.*

Lord Jesus, what words can express the gratitude that

wants to flow from my heart? Your grace is astounding. John Newton called it amazing. It is counterintuitive to my religious, performance-based flesh to believe the gospel. And yet, by your indwelling Spirit I can sing,

Amazing Grace, how sweet the sound, that saved a wretch like me! I once was lost but now am found, was blind, but now I see!

What I see is more of my sin—more of that for which you died, Jesus. Yes, let me be ever mindful of my unworthiness. But let me be even more aware of your atoning, cleansing blood—the blood that speaks of your love and grace and motivates me, with joyful humility, to live for the one to whom I so gladly and thankfully belong.

The Bronze Serpent

"And as Moses lifted up the serpent in the wilderness, so must the Son of Man be lifted up, what whoever believes in Him shall have eternal life."

John 3:14-15

. . . . ● ● ● ● ● ● ● ● ● . . . .

Father in heaven, many people are familiar with John 3:16. But the previous verses describe the image of the bronze serpent from Numbers 21, when the Israelites gave themselves to what they did best: grumble and complain against you and Moses. To teach them a sober lesson in their lack of faith and gratitude, and as an act of judgment, you sent venomous snakes into the camp. Many people were bitten and died. As one would expect, the rest of the community cried out for help. And in your great mercy, you responded by instructing Moses to forge a bronze serpent and place it high on a pole so that whenever anyone was bitten, he or she could look upon the image and live.

Lord Jesus, John records your teaching that Numbers 21 was a shadow of the cross. That you are the bronze serpent upon whom I must fix my eyes of faith. And just as the snake-bitten Israelites were to look to the serpent, sin-bitten folks like me are to look to you and *believe,* since I, too, am a grumbler and complainer just like the Israelites. I deserve judgment, but in your great mercy, you have given me grace.

Jesus, I am called to believe that what has killed my soul and separated me from the Father was injected into you like venom as an act of judgment upon my sinfulness. You received the justice of God so that I might receive the mercy of God, being counted as reconciled and righteous, adopted and accepted.

Paul says that even though you had never sinned, you became a sin substitute for me, so that I might become the righteousness of God through you. And now you call me to believe that truth. To rest and abide in it. To tie and tether my life to it.

I can imagine that some of the Israelites were skeptical of Moses' command to look upon a bronze snake to be healed. Look and live. Really? Father, my heart asks the same question. *Believe* and live? *Believe* and be forgiven? *Believe* and be reconciled. *Believe* and be counted *righteous.* Really? My head continues to rebel against the gospel, and my heart far too often remains skeptical and cynical of your offer of complete forgiveness.

Father, my prayer today is that you would give me the grace to believe the gospel. To really believe, rest and abide in Jesus. To know that my wounds are very real. They are fatal. But the gospel tells me that, by the wounds of my Savior, I am healed. It tells me that Jesus became a curse so that I might be blessed and a blessing. In the same way that the venom of sin brought death to Jesus, may the gospel be the anti-venom that brings life to all who believe—*to the praise of your glorious grace!*

About the Author

McKay Caston has been married for over twenty-eight years to a beautiful red head with whom he has been graced with three children. Having received B.A., M.Div., D.Min., and Ph.D. degrees, McKay has served as a pastor for over twenty-five years in role ranging from assistant pastor, to lead pastor, and most recently as founding pastor. He also has had the privilege of teaching on the faculty for Metro Atlanta Seminary and mentoring young pastors in The Timothy Fellowship.

For much of his life, McKay misinterpreted the gospel to be a form of moralism whereby God would accept and bless him based on his goodness (or at least if he looked better than others). He lived like the Jews in Romans 10:3, "Being ignorant of the righteousness that comes from God, and seeking to establish their own, they did not submit to God's righteousness."

However, over the years and by God's grace, he is growing in his understanding of the substitutionary nature of the cross, of the imputation of Jesus' righteousness, and of what it means to be a dearly loved, adopted child of God. These doctrines have become very precious to him, and now serve as the centerpiece of his ministry through *Rest for the Weary*.

Find more resources at www.restfortheweary.net.

Made in the USA
Columbia, SC
29 September 2020